THIS BOOK B

):

Bonjour, Ciao, Hola, hello. I'm Matt the cat — or Mateo, Matteo, Matheus, or Mathieu... depending on the vineyard. From Napa to Tuscany, we'll sip, color, and take it slow. Because good wine — and good days — aren't meant to be rushed.

-Matt, the Cat

Our refined cat sommelier, ever curious, samples the deep red nectar straight from the barrel using a wine thief—a slender glass pipette designed for tasting. With a discerning eye and a refined palate, he savors the bold, complex character that makes Bordeaux wines a global treasure.

FOOD PAIRING

The bold, tannic structure of Bordeaux complements the hearty flavors of slow-cooked beef like Beef Bourguignon.

The creamy, tangy notes of Roquefort
cheese pair well with depth of Bordeaux reds.

Pinot Noir's acidity and light tannins match the rich, savory flavors of Coq au Vin.

Époisses de Bourgogne Cheese

The creamy pungent flavor pairs beautifully with a glass
of earthy red Burgundy.

I'M NOT DRINKING ALONE IF THE CAT'S HOME.

–Matt, the Cat

AGED TO PURR-FECTION
INSPECTING THE FINEST CHAMPAGNE
Curiosity: Good champagne has fine, persistent bubbles that
rise slowly and don't dissipate quickly.

Champagne and caviar – a luxurious duo. The crisp bubbles enhance the rich, briny flavors, creating a perfect harmony.

Wine: because the cat's already judging you.

–Matt, the Cat

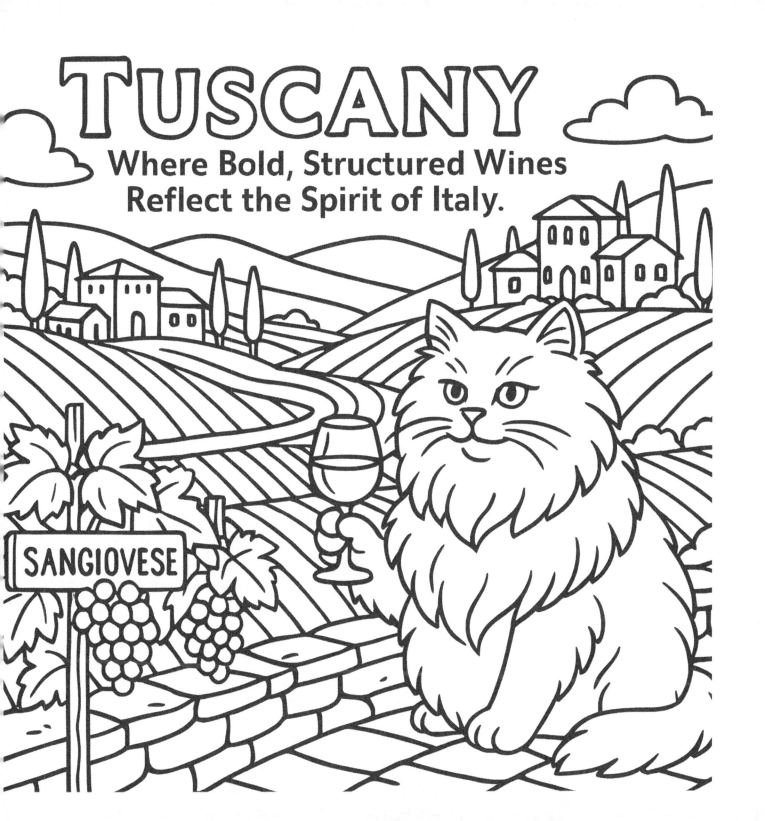

The hearty Bistecca alla Fiorentina pairs well with the rich tannins of Brunello.

You can't buy happiness, but you can buy wine–and I'll sit in the box it came in. –Matt, the Cat

Rioja, Spain
Home of Bold, Spicy Reds with Notes of Cherry and Leather

The smoky, spicy chorizo enhances **RIOJA'S** ROBUST FLAVOR PROFILE.

The acidity and spice of RIOJA balance the hearty, fried dish of *Patatas Bravas*

NAPA VALLEY, CALIFORNIA
The Home of Bold Cabernet and Refined Merlot.

Just Another Purrfect Day in Napa Valley

Bold, tangy blue cheese and Cabernet create a flavor explosion.

Napa Cabernet's tannins balance
the rich, meaty flavors of a grilled ribeye

Sonoma California

A Diverse Landscape for Pinot Noir and Chardonnay

Sonoma Chardonnay's acidity complements the rich, buttery salmon.

A bright Pinot Noir pairs well with the earthy, creamy goat cheese.

Mendoza

Bold, Fruity Malbec with a Touch of Spice.

Malbec's fruitiness and spice
complement the hearty, flavorful empanadas.

The bold, smoky flavors of Asado
pair perfectly with Mendoza's robust Malbec.

**Barossa Valley - Bold Shiraz
with rich peppery notes.**

Dark Chocolate and Barossa Valley–
–A Decadent Duo of Bold Flavors

Marlborough

Marlborough – Crisp Sauvignon Blanc with Zesty Grilled Shrimp

If you enjoyed this journey, don't miss Matt's first adventure - **_A Cat's Guide to the Good Life_** - a purrfect intro to living luxuriously, one nap at time.

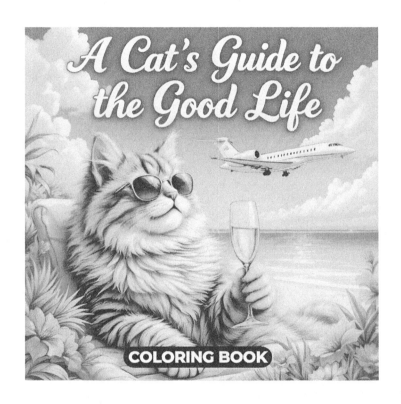

THANKS FOR COLORING WITH US!

LET'S KEEP IN TOUCH!

Follow us on Instagram
@achrcreative
and tag your artwork
with **#MattTheCat**.

Stay curious.
Stay cozy.
Stay cat-tastic.

With purrs and whiskers,
—Matt the Cat

Made in United States
Orlando, FL
30 April 2025

60899723R00057